A Voice in the Wilderness

A Voice in the Wilderness

Justin Farley

"Who are you?" He confessed, and did not deny, but confessed, "I am not the Christ." And they asked him, "What then? Are you Elijah?" He said, "I am not." "Are you the Prophet?" And he answered, "No." So they said to him, "Who are you? We need to give an answer to those who sent us. What do you say about yourself?" He said, "I am the voice of one crying out in the wilderness, 'Make straight the way of the Lord,' as the prophet Isaiah said."

John 1:19-23

We are all prophets with a voice calling out into the wilderness of this world. We all have been given unique talents and gifts to "prepare the way for the Lord"*. And it's time we all use them.

*Matthew 3:3

For the restless heart that wrestles and wonders

The Light that Shines in the Darkness

There's a light that shines in the darkness.
There's a destiny waiting at the end of the road.
There's meaning in the middle of this emptiness.
There's a reason you've been asked to bear this heavy load.

Lessons are taught when we reach out
Farther than we thought we'd ever dare.
Faith abounds when we confront our deepest doubts,
Enduring more than we dreamed we could ever bear.

There's a dawn waiting at the edge of every midnight.
There's a seed planted with every fallen leaf.
With every wrong, there's the chance to make a right.
With every hour of suffering, there's an eternity of relief.

Our darkest moments give us the opportunity
For seasons of our greatest growth.
Everyday we work towards continuity
Of acceptance and persistent hope.

And there's a light that shines in the darkness.
There's a star that guides the way.
There's a gate that's open to forgiveness.
There's a shepherd who saves those who've gone astray.

When Trouble Comes

Evening's crippling darkness passes away.
It's distant vigor muted by the beauty of the morn.
Hope shines forth from the sun's mighty rays,
A new spirit within us is born.

I am not overburdened by life's troubles.
Though painful, they'll not shackle nor strangle me.
For each of life's daily struggles
Provide growth's greatest opportunity.

When the seas of my demise rise
And the wake of fear crests beyond the levee's peak,
Faith persists and finds a way to uphold and drive
Me just beyond the tide of trouble's reach.

We are neither all dark nor light—
We're destined to reside somewhere in-between.
Constantly conscious of the ongoing fight,
Casting our character in each of life's scenes.

We can't prevent the sun from sleeping
Nor hide from life's inevitable dark and lonesome night.
But we can cling to a hope never fleeting
When joy seems unattainable and out of sight.

It's in consistently choosing not to settle
That we become flowers and not merely dormant seeds.
And yet, we're still fragile petals—
Wisdom means learning to sway with life's breeze.

Cosmic Love

Stepping stone across the river of life,
You provide light beneath the cloak of night.

Safe harbor upon the rocky sea,
You are the greatest hope residing within me.

Epic wonder, woven tapestry of mystique,
You are the answer all my questions seek.

Cup of mercy and revitalizing love,
You are beyond what minds can conceive of.

Oh, highest virtue! Oh, redeemer of the lost flock!
You open the doors of death that once were locked.

Microscopic nothing compared to your vast size;
Cosmic everything in the sight of your eyes.

If Even...

If even the song of a sparrow
can uplift a heavy heart,
what excuse can I give
to not play my part?

If even the waters of the river
without hands or feet can move stone,
what reasoning can I use
to conclude I'm incapable and forlorn?

If even tiny ants roaming the kitchen
can walk off with a waiting meal,
how much more strength resides within me
to help, console, and heal?

If even the wings of a butterfly
can marvel and mystify the mind,
imagine the power we all hold
to transform and mend mankind.

Hell

Stairs descend the realm of Earth
and end in pits devoid of beauty,
built upon the belief that
our failures deem us unworthy.
Sin's aim is to convince the heart
that we've forfeited our right
to be looked upon with love
and affection in God's sight.

But the halls of hell
are walled with portraits we've painted,
tainted by brushes dripping
with fear, guilt, and shame.
We are not without blame,
but in our minds' motif of damnation,
we omit our Father's fundamental disposition
towards love, forgiveness, and mercy.
And thus, leave the wellspring of life still thirsty,
believing we are unworthy
of a drink,
never stopping to think
and meditate on the Cross
and how much he loves us.

Jehovah-Rapha
The Lord Who Heals

I've felt the heat of your Spirit burn within me,
felt your breath blow on my heart
like a pair of bellows,
providing oxygen for glowing embers of love,
replacing cold, lifeless coals.

You've cultivated this barren soul
and labored with the persistence of a gardener,
clearing the weeds from my land
and continuing to pluck them by hand
each time a new one pops up.

You've pruned the dead weight from my branches,
chopped off my worldly distractions
in order to yield more fruit.
You've provided rich, black soil to grow roots of patience
where there was once rash temperament without restraint.

Your loving hands have lifted a head hung low in shame,
while your fierce winds have blown like a tornado,
leveling the walls of pride I constructed.
These walls I thought were so strong now crumble
beneath the weight of your glory.

You've provided real safety for me in a solid fortress
with ramparts tall and wide,
and I reside deep within the heart of your city.
Sufferings of this world are felt
but never dwell in my stronghold.

You've blessed me with the gift of wisdom,
taught me to pause and sow seeds of contemplation -
I once dove headfirst into life's battles
like a torpedo of chaos without thought
only to be whipped into retreat, anxiously seeking cover.

Tongues of fire have rested on closed eyelids,
consuming this narrow vision of life revolved around me.
Your healing kiss has restored sight to a blind man;
I'm now able to see beyond the ego
and what it means to be called into servanthood.

Your loving discipline has produced humility
capable of creating laughter
when I take myself too seriously,
caught up in grandiose schemes and dreams
of personal glory.

You've implanted fragments of courage in me.
Each day it's easier to strip off these clothes of delusion
and encourage the world to look at my naked frame—
imperfect, bound by my weaknesses,
yet liberated by your name.

You've taught me how to sow
where I once only reaped.
Tiny seeds of faith have sprouted hope,
setting my heart on distant destinations
where not long ago I accepted defeat.

The Spirit moves at an incalculable pace,
a pace beyond human comprehension.
You are the tortoise and the hare.
Sometimes dashing and overwhelming.
Sometimes sluggish and barely felt moving at all.

Faith has given me footsteps
where my feet were once immobile, heavy as iron.
Fear remains, but it no longer incapacitates me.
When my vision remains focused on you,
I can walk on water.

I'm no longer afraid of my mind's questions.
You've given me the green light
to doubt, to challenge, to investigate, to reason;
but you've also allowed my heart to accept
that a spiritual walk requires steps of blind faith.

It's becoming easier to call you Captain
and turn over my position to you at the helm,
finally able to accept I'm incapable of navigating this ship,
understanding that you're the only one
qualified to direct the course of my life.

Your affirmed grace eases my mind over finite time.
My soul once restlessly rattled the cage of the body,
unceasingly banged upon the heavy door of immortality,
pleading for an escape from death
and the plague of old age.

But you make peace of mind a possible reality,
detached from the bondage of the self
and starved of the selfish desires of the flesh.
You give me food filled with substance,
where I once only chewed and swallowed emptiness.

I am far from peace.
I am not absent of fear.
I am still riddled by questions without answers.
I am still moved by my sufferings.
I come unhinged by my madness.
I am inhibited by narcissistic thoughts.
I waver under trials.
I have moments of doubt.
I still unsheathe my tongue as a weapon.
I still have days where my patience runs short.
I am sometimes guarded and seek solitude instead of love.
I am still annoyed when others need my hand or my time.
I still fall prey to temptations.

Yes, I admit that I am far from perfect.
But your perfection is constant within me,
everyday molding and shaping me into a better man.

Mistakes and Promises

My mistakes are too great to measure,
my promises can collapse under pressure,
and I still fall prey to desire,
enticed by those same, old lies
time and time again.

But when the waves of sin pass,
guilt juts through my soul like shards of glass,
and I'm left brooding over these deep moral wounds
that I continually pick the scabs off of,
yet all the while praying they will heal.

The paradox of the heart is puzzling,
for the evidence is overwhelming
that man can't even trust himself
to uphold his own standard of righteousness,
let alone the commandments of God.

So the ladder to Heaven looms high —
a daunting force towering in the sky —
leaving these fractured bones aching
at the thought of making the climb
and conquering these demons I shamefully
find pleasing in my ears.

The baggage is too heavy to carry;
our errors are too large to bury,
but the Lord knew our battle was lost before it had begun.
He mercifully stepped into our place,
wiped the stain of sin from our fate,
and washed us in the redeeming river of his love.

My mistakes are too great to measure,
my promises can collapse under pressure,
but the only promise I need is found in Christ,
whose wildfire of love engulfs my mistakes
and gives me the grace
to continue walking with God.

The Black Veil

I wear this black veil of despair
like the wrappings of a mummy,
covering my soul's deep-seated wounds.

My face frozen in cold, blank stare
trapped within my tomb—
here, alone in my room.

Why do you continue to test me?
Why do you hold out savory meat
only to snatch it from my hands?

It is wrong for me to question your authority,
to question the goodness of your plans,
to hold you in contempt, unable to understand?

I wear this lonely shroud of betrayal.
Spend my days wondering
why I'm the one being denied.

Haven't I sought to be faithful?
Why are the wicked given an easy ride,
never facing near my trials nor the tears I've cried?

I wear this black veil of despair,
but I trust that you know more
than what sits before my somber scene.

Despite my suffering, the Cross tells me you care
so be my rock upon which I lean
no matter what plays upon life's screen.

The Lamp Light

The lamp light is lit.
The atoning flame burns
through the tar of my sin
and spreads a blazing fire within my heart.
I am mesmerized as knowledge becomes wisdom—
the calming vision that you lay upon my eyes.
Tear down these fragile, crumbling walls of pride.
Replace them with stones that reach up to the heavens,
and completely rebuild me on the inside.
Lord, build me a fortress of faith.
that is impenetrable, insurmountable, and indestructible.

Free me from my own destruction,
and protect me from the forces of delusion
that come knocking at the gate,
coaxing me into embracing the world's desires
and eroding my faith.
I hear them whispering their lies...
You're a prisoner who must be set free.
Embrace your desires. Don't you want to be happy?
But grant me the eyes to see
through the tricks of temptation.
Assure my soul that there is
only one road towards salvation;
the walk of faith is arduous and lonely,
yet it's life's most rewarding journey
because it is so.

Allow me to know your will when confusion seizes me,
and my will fights with all its might to cling to
what is temporal, easy, and immediately gratifying.
Keep this lamp lit, and may its flame never wane
or dim against the breeze of change
or the winds of the world.
May I call you Lord not simply in word alone
but recognize, answer to, and serve you
as a slave to a master.
When disaster strikes,
prevent my fear from persuading me
to cut off these cords
and to put myself back into control.
May your lamp light my way
through the often dark and confusing forest.
May its fires warm and heat my soul
in a blaze of your immeasurable glory.
And may I live, desiring only to live out your plans,
and not to write my own story.

A Voice in the Wilderness

There's a voice in the wilderness
that's only silence to the ears,
but the broken heart hears
a soothing voice of redemption and hope.

There's a voice in the wilderness
that quakes with a thundering rumble,
that shakes the stubborn soul lowly and humble,
that opens blind eyes with a holy roar.

There's a voice in the wilderness
that offers grace and mercy
to the sinner desolate and thirsty
for forgiveness, for a fresh start.

Listen…

Hear the voice in your wilderness.
Your maker calls in the midst of your trials
and trudges with you along life's lonely miles.
Hear your lover calling your name.

Everyday Miracles

The clamor of your wisdom claps
like a thousand hands in unison throughout the forest,
calling from every treetop
and whispering within every breath the wind blows.
Your Spirit is found in the simplicity of a dew drop
and in the caws of a congregation of crows.

You are an invisible hand,
opening and closing doors as you see fit—
not always on my time frame,
not always giving me access to the rooms I wish,
but often I find ignorance is bliss.
For you block my most cherished paths,
knowing they only lead into an eternal abyss.

You are the Wise King,
always leading, but serving simultaneously.
With each new day you birth into existence,
I am astonished at your beauty.
You're never hard to find
when my awareness is focused on you
and turned away from the desires of my mind.

Your miracles come in small packages,
constantly sent, but rarely opened.
I look for you in grandiose experiences,
but you keep gently tugging at my sleeve,
urging me to put on my leather gloves
and dig for you in the dirt of the garden.

If I'm not careful,
I can become oblivious to the everyday mystery —
the beauty of a daffodil,
the way sunlight rests upon my windowsill,
the Spirit who speaks when my mind gets still,
and the non-coincidental meetings of strangers,
sharing the exact conversations I need to hear.

Open my eyes when they are blind to your majesty,
so that I may witness your glory
in every root, rock, river, and ravine.
May I read the love letters you've written
upon every stump I pass in the forest,
every deer that crosses my path,
and every squirrel that leaps from limb to limb.

And may I marvel at your everyday miracles
and find your fingerprints
upon every piece of evidence
in this case called life.

Grace

I am awed by the way you move me,
leading me like fluttering snowflakes
that follow the direction of the wind.
Some days I forget the barren tundra
from which I came and how you whispered my name
echoing across that vacant landscape
in a gentle, yet incessant cadence
that was unable to be ignored.

Some days pass without me even once remembering
that each moment is a treasure —
a gift freely given, light years away from being deserved.
But despite all my wrongs
and all the foolish footpaths I've walked,
in my time of desperation I called out to you
and without hesitation you answered.

Every single second contains abounding opportunity —
a renewed possibility for a changed life.
I was unable to arrive at my destination
by the work of my own hands,
but while I lingered, withering away in the darkness,
you tucked me under your wing
and brought me back into the light.

The fact that I breathe and my heart beats
is a living testament to your endless love and grace.
May I never forget the prison and chaos
of that distant past, living a life separated from you.
May I forever remember that you rescued me
from the shadow of myself
and that each day is a gift
that I should never waste
and unceasingly praise you for.

Upon This Rock

Upon this rock I live
uncertain yet composed.
Not crushed beneath the veil of darkness —
within me there's a light that glows.
Demons harass me with my weaknesses,
using past failures to breed fear of future plans.
But upon this rock I'm free —
caressed and cradled in loving hands.
I'm often startled by my actions;
they belong to someone holier than the man I know.
But God redeems even our darkest ways
when we accept his command to follow.
Selfishness still has moments of victory,
but sin only makes me more in awe of his grace.
For the Spirit now resides within me,
and old desires have been replaced.
It's by no strong will of mine
but because of this rock on which I stand.
It's only by the power of the Divine
that I'm being transformed into a better man.

Hide and Seek

One.
Two.
Three...
One-hundred.
Ready or not, here I come.

Just where could you be hiding?
Your favorite spots could be endless
across an ever-expanding universe.

Are you crouching within a crater on the moon?
Riding around the rings of Saturn
like a spinning merry-go-round?
Swirling within the storms of Jupiter?
Getting a tan upon the surface of Venus?
Swimming through the Milky Way
like a breakfast grain in a bowl of cereal?

Or maybe farther yet,
out across seas of space and time,
multitudes of galaxies Magellan
would have loved to sail and navigate?

Oh, the quest is hopeless.
I search and search,
overturning each and every rock
but never even find a clue.

I must admit...
you're quite the funny fellow.
I imagine your grin stretches
across the black void of space.

You must get a chuckle and kick
out of human ignorance
because each time I resolve to quit
this game, you show up unexpectedly,
tapping me on the shoulder
and staying just long enough
to convince me that you're not done playing.
And the game begins again.

But this game has lasted for years.
The lines and rules have become blurred.
I no longer know who's hiding and who's seeking.
Maybe I've limited my vision to cosmic proportions,
so I could convince myself that even if I found you,
you'd be too far away to reach anyways...
Maybe the jokes on me...
Maybe I'm the one who's been hiding all along...

But what if you're here,
right now,
on this very page,
trying to get my attention that the jig is up,
that I've been found —
that, in fact, I was never hidden to begin with?

You just loved me enough
to give me the opportunity to believe I was,
while you've patiently waited outside the closet door
like a loving parent longing to greet me
on the day I'm finally ready to be found.

One.
Two.
Three…
One-hundred.
Ready or not, here I come.